D0995116

half-caste

For Simon Powell

half-caste

JOHN AGARD

Hodder
Children's
Books

HODDER CHILDREN'S BOOKS

First published in Great Britain in 2004 by Hodder Children's Books
This paperback edition first published in 2013
This edition published in 2017 by Hodder and Stoughton

10 9 8 7

Text copyright © John Agard, 2004

The moral rights of the author have been asserted.

A CIP catalogue record for this book
is available from the British Library.

ISBN 978 0340 89389 0

Printed and bound in Great Britain by Clays Ltd, Elcograf S.p.A.

The paper and board used in this book are made from wood from responsible sources

MIX
Paper from
responsible sources
FSC
www.fsc.org   FSC® C104740

Hodder Children's Books
An imprint of Hachette Children's Group
Part of Hodder & Stoughton
Carmelite House
50 Victoria Embankment
London EC4Y 0DZ

Acknowledgements: poems on pages 11, 21, 26, 27, 30, 34, 40, 55
60, 67 – from *Get Back Pimple* (Penguin Viking 1996); 14, 50 – from
Mangoes & Bullets (Serpent's Tail 1990); 52 – from *Hello H2O*
(Hodder Wayland 2003); 28 – from *A Stone's Throw From
Embankment* (Royal Festival Hall 1993); 64 – from *Bard At The
Beeb* (BBC Learning Support 1998); 43 – from *From The Devil's
Pulpit* (Bloodaxe Books 1997); 63 – from *Upon Westminster Bridge*,
edited by Alice and Peter Oswald (The Wordsworth Trust, 2002).

A Note From the Author

Readers often assume that when a poet uses 'I' in a poem, then it must be about the poet himself or herself. Since I only became familiar with the expression 'half-caste' after moving to Britain, it is not meant to be autobiographical. But I wanted to give a voice to 'half-caste', and through a series of absurd images point to the absurdity of perceiving a human being in terms of 'halves'. So when Tchaikovsky, for instance, mixes a black key with a white key, is the result a half-caste symphony? When light and shadow mix in the sky, is the result a half-caste weather?

Behind the poem lies the harsh lesson of history that the obsession with purity can lead to genocide. The satirical tone of the poem, you can put down to my inspiration from calypso, a powerful Caribbean musical genre in which mischievous lyrics take on serious issues.

I hope you enjoy the collection and grow up not to 'half' a future, but to a full life enriched by the wonder of human diversity. Remember, poetry can be your ally along the way.

Contents

And All Was Good 8

My Move Your Move 9

Union Jack And Union Jill 10

Half-caste 11

Rainbow 14

Tongue 16

A Word 18

Message From Your Mobile 19

Right-On Mr Left 20

Smoke-Loving Girl Blues 21

Angels For Neighbours 23

Flag 24

A Vampire's Priorities 25

A Hello From Cello 26

The Hurt Boy And The Birds 27

Boomerang 28

That Mouth 29

Behold My Pen 30

Punctuating The Silence 32

Poetry Jump-Up 34

Follow That Steel Pan 37

Coal's Son And Diamond's Daughter 39

A Date With Spring 40

Vote For Your Local Shadow	42
Twins	43
Quest	45
Clouds	47
The Ozone Liar	48
Cowtalk	50
Who'll Save Dying Man?	52
For The Record	54
One Question From A Bullet	55
A Hand On A Forehead	56
Not Arms	57
Checking Out Me History	60
Toussaint L'Overture Acknowledges Wordsworth's Sonnet 'To Toussaint L'Overture'	63
Windrush Child	64
Crybaby Prime Minister	67
Skin	69
A Social Skeleton	71
The Giant With A Taste For Mongrel Blood	73
Behind The Menu	74
Salt	76
Coal	77
Marriage Of Opposites	78
Notes	80

And All Was Good

If I were maker of the human race
I'd give each one a rainbow face.

How about one eye red, one eye yellow,
And two cheeks of indigo.

A violet nose that sticks out in profile.
Orange lips to strike a smile.

A pair of blue eyebrows would be fitting.
Green eyelashes for flitting.

I'll breathe the spectrum into the features
Of these, my new-fashioned creatures.

I'll say: 'Even if you can't see eye-to-eye,
At least, go forth and multiply.'

Then I'll have a well-earned seventh day rest,
Cock my feet up, having set the world to right.

I'll read the Sunday papers to keep abreast
Of happenings in black and white.

My Move Your Move

Blacks have their castles.
Whites have their castles.
Blacks have their knights.
Whites have their knights.
Blacks have their pawns.
Whites have their pawns.

A white queen mates a black king.
A black queen mates a white king.
All done from an improbable position
with a bit of polite parrying.
And nobody mentions equal rights.

It's a game of royal composition,
where even the air seems self-possessed.
The clock ticks, the brain cells tingle.
And yet grandmaster, Kasparov, calls chess
'a black and white jungle'.

Well, if chess's squares are ruled by tooth and claw,
do forgive me if I eat your bishop raw.

Union Jack And Union Jill

Union Jack
and Union Jill
went up the hill
for a patriotic fling.

One waved a flag
and marched up and down.
One sang an anthem
and saluted after.

But they stole a quick kiss
as they talked politics
and soon love grew taller
than their raised fists.

For Union Jack
and Union Jill
the grass stood still
the hill hoisted its bliss

And they rolled over
in a peel of laughter
to find their convictions
all flying in tatters.

Half-caste

Excuse me
standing on one leg
I'm half-caste

Explain yuself
wha yu mean
when yu say half-caste
yu mean when picasso
mix red an green
is a half-caste canvas/
explain yuself
wha yu mean
when yu say half-caste
yu mean when light an shadow
mix in de sky
is a half-caste weather/
well in dat case
england weather
nearly always half-caste
in fact some o dem cloud
half-caste till dem overcast
so spiteful dem don't want de
  sun pass
ah rass/
explain yuself

wha yu mean

when yu say half-caste

yu mean when tchaikovsky

sit down at dah

    piano

and mix a black key

wid a white key

is a half-caste symphony/

Explain yuself

wha yu mean

Ah listening to yu wid de keen

half of mih ear

Ah looking at yu wid de keen

half of mih eye

an when I'm introduced to you

I'm sure you'll understand

why I offer yu half-a-hand

an when I sleep at night

I close half-a-eye

consequently when I dream

I dream half-a-dream

an when moon begin

  to glow

I half-caste human being
cast half-a-shadow
but yu must come back tomorrow

wid de whole of yu eye
an de whole of yu ear
an de whole of yu mind

an I will tell yu
de other half
of my story

Rainbow

When you see
de rainbow
you know
God know
wha he doing –
one big smile
across the sky –
I tell you
God got style
the man got style

When you see
raincloud pass
and de rainbow
make a show
I tell you
is God doing
limbo
the man doing
limbo

But sometimes

you know

when I see

de rainbow

so full of glow

& curving

like she bearing child

I does want know

if God

ain't a woman

If that is so

the woman got style

man she got style

Tongue

Small flame
under the roof
of a mouth.
You devour
You cleanse
You tell honey
from vinegar.
You speak truth.
You speak slander.
You soothe
with a kiss.
You bruise
with a word.

To the possessed
you are the gift
of enlightenment.
To the dispossessed
you are the scale
of judgement.

Small flame
under the roof
of a mouth.

Tyranny knows
your hiding place.

A Word

A word
can turn
a key
in a door
or a knife
through a heart.

A word
can touch
with the chill
of ice
or be all
the more nice
for saying
sweet nothing.

Message From
Your Mobile

I am the message-bringer
who leans against yr cheek.
I bridge the distance.
I lord it over yr silence.

Some dare to call me nuisance
But I announce my presence

As I make public private thoughts.
I expose the one-to-one.
I transport lovers' sweet murmurs.
I guard the dying's last words.

Leave a message after the tone.
I'll text yr flesh and bone.

Right-On Mr Left

Keep on searching for Mr Right.
Somewhere out there there's Mr Right.
I've got nothing against Mr Right.
But what if you miss Mr Right?
Have you considered Mr Left?
Haven't you left out Mr Left?
Somewhere out there there's Mr Left.
What if Mr Left turns out
to be none other than Mr Right?
Will it be love at first sight?
Will the earth move, will the stars dance,
if the right mood and circumstance
united Miss Right and Mr Left?
What if Mr Left longed for Miss Left?
What if Miss Left still longed for Mr Right?

Smoke-Loving Girl Blues

Would like her for my girlfriend any day
Would follow if she showed the way
Would feel honoured if she be my queen

But she's a smoke-loving girl
And I'm allergic to nicotine

Would wheel with her on the ice-skating rink
Would fall with her over the brink
Would stare with her bewitched and serene

But she's a smoke-loving girl
And I'm allergic to nicotine

Would give her my last polo mint
Would hit the skies if she gave me a hint
Would do anything even dye my hair green

But she's a smoke-loving girl
And I'm allergic to nicotine

Would lay down my jacket for her gorgeous feet
Would fan her cheeks to keep away the heat
Would shine her shoes till she's lost in the sheen

But she's a smoke-loving girl
And I'm allergic to nicotine

Lawd now my head is in a haze
Cause of that girl and her smoke-loving ways

Angels For Neighbours

If you want a neighbour from hell,
try living next door to an angel.
Not that I mind the occasional choir,
but there's so much a man can take
of way-past-midnight harps and lyres,
not to mention trumpet blasts and wings
fluttering in the wee hours of morning.
To be fair, angels do have their good points:
Angels don't throw beer cans over the hedge.
Angels don't leave condoms littering the lawn.
Angels don't urinate on garden gnomes.
Angels don't go around mugging old ladies.
Yet a part of me keeps thinking:
What if these cherubim and seraphim
started dressing in denim
and making for our mortal sons and daughters?
What if these so-called divine messengers
had their sights set on taking over?
What if people like you and me
were the only ones on the street without wings?

Flag

What's that fluttering in a breeze?
It's just a piece of cloth
that brings a nation to its knees.

What's that unfurling from a pole?
It's just a piece of cloth
that makes the guts of men grow bold.

What's that rising over a tent?
It's just a piece of cloth
that dares the coward to relent.

What's that flying across a field?
It's just a piece of cloth
that will outlive the blood you bleed.

How can I possess such a cloth?
Just ask for a flag, my friend.
Then blind your conscience to the end.

A Vampire's Priorities

Today I want to do green things.

Eavesdrop on the gossip of leaves.

Tune in to the voices of trees.

Translate every whisper of grass.

Put myself in the place of spring.

Even something as simple

as eat a granny smith apple.

Today I want to do green things.

But there are red things to be done.

A rose to savour.

A flame to tend to.

Another throat to treasure.

A Hello From Cello

Stroke
me
high
Stroke
me
low
with a ripple of your bow
till my plump body
begins to glow
with the O-so-sweet harmony.
Make me hum make me buzz make me drone.
Rest my slender neck beside your own.
Close me in the secret of your lap
till fall curtain and fade clap.
Remember my ornate toe will be curled
like a rude question mark
against the applause in your ear.
I may even whisper four-letter words
such as
Bach
Aria
Opus

.
.
.

The Hurt Boy And The Birds

The hurt boy talked to the birds
and fed them the crumbs of his heart.

It was not easy to find the words
for secrets he hid under his skin.
The hurt boy spoke of a bully's fist
that made his face a bruised moon –
his spectacles stamped to ruin.

It was not easy to find the words
for things that nightly hissed
as if his pillow was a hideaway for creepy-crawlies –
the note sent to the girl he fancied
held high in mockery.

But the hurt boy talked to the birds
and their feathers gave him welcome –

Their wings taught him new ways to become.

Boomerang

Featherless bird
I will nest in the eye of wind

Crescent moon
fashioned by hand
I will slice the sky of your gaze

Crooked stick
I will aspire to the gift of wings

Rainbow wood
I will bridge what is and is not imagined
forever curving towards the path of origin

Hurl me from your hand. But
remember.
I am the dream the wind has
given you.

That Mouth

That mouth
was generous with kisses.

That mouth
was rich with tall tales.

That mouth
was at home with grapes.

That mouth
was a wealth of jokes.

Now that mouth
will say no more.

will laugh no more.
And the silence hurts.

Behold My Pen

Behold my pen
my pen is a friend
that cries
blue tears
on the cheek
of a page

Behold my pen
my pen is a friend
that flies
across the cloud
of a page

Behold my pen

my pen is a friend

that spies

a face

in the mirror

of a page

Behold my pen

my pen is a friend

that sometimes

writes truth

sometimes lies

How do I dare erase

the footprints of my friend?

Punctuating The Silence

I could be a comma,
and pause you
in mid-sentence

I could be an exclamation!
and make an exhibition
of myself

I could be a full stop.
And halt you
in your tracks

I could be quotation marks
inverted commas if you like
and 'box in' your speech

Or even a question mark?
and teach
by posing no answer

I'll settle for a dash –
marry myself
to Emily Dickinson's ghost

becoming a passing footprint
a tiny black bridge
between one imponderable

and another

Poetry Jump-Up

Tell me if Ah seeing right
Take a look down de street

w^{o}r$_d$$_s$ d$_a$n^c^{i}n
w^{o}r$_d$$_s$ d$_a$n^c$_i$n
till dey sweat
words like fishes
jumpin out a net
words wild and free
joinin de poetry revelry
words back to back
words belly to belly

Come on everybody
come and join de poetry band
dis is poetry carnival
dis is poetry bacchanal
when inspiration call
take yu pen in yu hand
if yu don't have a pen
take yu pencil in yu hand

if you don't have a pencil

what the hell

so long de feeling start to swell

just shout de poem out

Words jumpin off de page

tell me if Ah seeing right

words like birds

jumpin out a cage

take a look down de street

words shakin dey waist

words shakin dey bum

words wit black skin

words wit white skin

words wit brown skin

words wit no skin at all

words huggin up words

an sayin I want to be a poem today

rhyme or no rhyme

I is a poem today

I mean to have a good time

Words feeling hot hot hot
big words feeling hot hot hot
lil words feeling hot hot hot
even sad words cant help
tappin dey toe
to de riddum of de poetry band

Dis is poetry carnival
dis is poetry bacchanal
so come on everybody
join de celebration
all yu need is plenty perspiration
an a little inspiration
plenty perspiration
an a little inspiration

Follow That Steel Pan

for Aubrey Bryan

Was a sledge hammer sink um down
to shape the belly of the sound
in a shanty town/
      with a boom-boom-boom
      from a fifty-five gallon oil drum

And a god named Ogun
take up a position
on a throne of iron/
      with a boom-boom-boom
      from a fifty-five gallon oil drum

And a spider named Nansi
guide the notes round
and dark metal was the loom/
      with a boom-boom-boom
      from a fifty-five gallon oil drum

And chisel follow chalk
where the notes lay down
and hammer follow chisel hum/
      with a boom-boom-boom
      from a fifty-five gallon oil drum

And tight was the steel
when fire stretch um/
And sweet was the feel
when water cool um/
And deep was the ping-pong
when two stick hit um/
And healing was the sound
when history hear um/

And it all began/
  with a boom-boom-boom
  from a fifty-five gallon oil drum/
  with a boom-boom-boom
  from a fifty-five gallon oil drum.

Coal's Son And Diamond's Daughter

Coal's son
and Diamond's daughter
were head over heels
in smouldering glittering love.
But the two families weren't keen.

The Coals
reminded their boy
of his ancient ancestry –
a glowing descendent
of fossilised plants.

The Diamonds
reminded their girl
of her crystal nature –
a sparkling example
of the hardest substance.

But Coal's son
and Diamond's daughter
embraced their atoms,
for their love went deeper
than a ring of carbon.

A Date With Spring

Got a date with Spring
Got to look me best.
Of all the trees
I'll be the smartest dressed.

Perfumed breeze
behind me ear.
Pollen accessories
all in place.
Raindrop moisturizer
for me face.
Sunlight tints
to spruce up the hair.

What's the good of being a tree
if you can't flaunt your beauty?

Winter, I was naked.
Exposed as can be.
Me wardrobe took off
with the wind.
Life was a frosty slumber.
Now, Spring, here I come.
Can't wait to slip in
to me little green number.

Vote For Your Local Shadow

Shadows appointed
Shadows reshuffled
Shadows with briefcases
Shadows in high places.

Shadows on the box
Shadows in the news
Shadows in living rooms
Shadows laying down rules.

Shadows with white papers
Shadows with blueprints
Shadows fed agendas
Shadows giving orders

Shadows deliberating
Shadows dictating
Shadows making promises
Shadows mouthing a text

Shadows we bless with an X.

Twins

To bring forth one
is to be blessed.

To bring forth two
is to be twice blessed.

But to bring forth
one black one white

twinned in the same womb
where day and night are one

(now here's a fine kettle
of genetic fish).

That is to enthrone
the miraculous mischief

of ovum and sperm
made flesh and bone.

That is to relearn
the lesson of the Ark –

raven and dove released
from love's tremulous flood.

Quest

Go south

Go north

Go east

Go west.

Still can't find God's address.

Go wake

Go dream

Go mountain

Go stream.

Still can't find God's address.

Go tree

Go stone

Go womb

Go bone.

Still can't find God's address.

Go forest

Go city

Go church

Go charity.

Still can't find God's address.

It wasn't that God
had moved out.
It was just that God
had moved in –
that place called myself.

Clouds

Those high-flying dragons
that are now here, now gone.

Those billowing maps
that know no boundaries.

Those candyfloss cities
that fade into the forgotten.

Those fluffy armies
that march into oblivion.

Not simply air pressure
or condensation of vapour.

But overhead reminders
of how the mighty rise and fall.

Divine graffiti
on sky's ever shifting wall.

The Ozone Liar

The ozone liar
says all is well with
the ozone layer.
The ozone liar
says chemicals won't harm
the ozone layer –
this fragile shield
of colourless gas
that protects
planet earth
from the sun's
ultra-violet.

The ozone liar
says waste won't harm
the ozone layer
or over-warm
the air we breathe
or stunt the forest
or grieve the sea.
The ozone liar
looks beyond the skies
to the stratosphere
and hides his eyes
from the fumes
of truth.

Cowtalk

Take a walk to the splendid morning fields of summer
check out the cows in full gleam
of their black and white hide

and remember was a man once say I have a dream
but they shoot him down in cold blood of day
because he had a mountaintop dream
of black and white hand in hand

take a walk to the splendid morning fields of summer
check out the cows in the green of meditation
a horde of black and white harmony

Maybe the cows trying to tell us something
but we the human butchers cant understand cowtalk
much less cowsilence
to interpret cowsilence you must send for a poet
not a butcher or a politician

cows in the interwoven glory
of their black and white hide
have their own mysterious story
cows in the interwoven glory

of their black and white hide

never heard of apartheid

never practise genocide

never seem to worry

that the grass greener on the other side

cows calmly marry and intermarry

cows in the interwoven glory

of their black and white hide

cows in the interwoven glory

of black and white integration

can't spell integration

cows never went to school

that's why cows so cool supercool

cows have little time for immigration rule

and above all cows never impose

their language on

another nation

do yoo mOO my message do yoo mOO

Who'll Save Dying Man?

Who'll save dying Man?
  I, said the Baboon.
Transplant my bone marrow,
and he'll wake tomorrow.

Who'll save dying Man?
  I, said the Chimpanzee.
He's welcome to my brain,
for deep down we're the same.

Who'll save dying Man?
  I, said the Pig.
I'll give him my liver.
May he live forever.

Who'll save dying Man?
  I, said the Sheep.
Let him have my kidney,
and that would be for free.

Who'll save dying Man?
  I, said the Rat.
My retina would do
to make his vision new.

Who'll save dying Man?
   I, said the Squid.
He can have our nerve cells,
for sea-folk wish him well.

Who'll save dying Man?
   I, said the Physician.
I'll save him with my skills,
though dying Man once killed.

'Thanks for the offer,'
   said dying Man.
'But I'd like to request
a Dodo for a doner.'

And the animals fell
a-whispering secretly:
   'O dying Man
has lost his memory.'

For The Record

The flea gives
the hedgehog
stimulation.
The hedgehog
provides the flea
with free
incubation.
This is just
a bit
of useless
information
on the subject
of co-operation.

One Question From A Bullet

I want to give up being a bullet
I've been a bullet too long

I want to be an innocent coin
in the hand of a child
and be squeezed through the slot
of a bubblegum machine

I want to give up being a bullet
I've been a bullet too long

I want to be a good luck seed
lying idle in somebody's pocket
or some ordinary little stone
on the way to becoming an earring
or just lying there unknown
among a crowd of other ordinary stones

I want to give up being a bullet
I've been a bullet too long

The question is
Can you give up being a killer?

A Hand On A Forehead

You don't have to be a refugee on a bus
from Zepa to Zenica
to understand that in the grammar of grief,
loss is not a noun
but an eternal verb.
And when words desert us,
the doing of a hand on a forehead,
besieged by memory,
bears witness to all frontlines
crosses all frontiers
speaks all mother tongues.
When the brain becomes a battleground,
and the past insists
on being the present tense,
a hand on a forehead needs no translator.

Not Arms

Not arms
that come
to kill
or maim

but arms
that hug
you closer
to your name

and offer
shelter
from hunger's
embrace

that hope
may enter
as a guest.

Not arms
that come
to silence
the dispossessed

but arms
that nurse
the roots
to harvest

and coax
water
from stony
ground

that grain
may share
its golden gift.

Not arms
that come
to talk
with bullets' tongue

but arms
that fathom
the source
of pain

that song

may return

to listening ear

as common

language

that knows

no frontier.

Checking Out Me History

Dem tell me
Dem tell me
Wha dem want to tell me

Bandage up me eye with me own history
Blind me to me own identity

Dem tell me bout 1066 and all dat
dem tell me bout Dick Whittington and he cat
But Toussaint L'Ouverture
no dem never tell me bout dat

    Toussaint
    a slave
    with vision
    lick back
    Napoleon
    battalion
    and first Black
    Republic born
    Toussaint de thorn
    to de French
    Toussaint de beacon
    of de Haitian Revolution

Dem tell me bout de man who discover de balloon
and de cow who jump over de moon
Dem tell me bout de dish run away with de spoon
but dem never tell me bout Nanny de maroon

>Nanny
>See-far woman
>of mountain dream
>fire-woman struggle
>hopeful stream
>to freedom river

Dem tell me bout Lord Nelson and Waterloo
but dem never tell me bout Shaka de great Zulu
Dem tell me bout Columbus and 1492
but what happen to de Caribs and de Arawaks too

Dem tell me bout Florence Nightingale and she lamp
and how Robin Hood used to camp
Dem tell me bout ole King Cole was a merry ole soul
but dem never tell me bout Mary Seacole

>From Jamaica
>she travel far

to the Crimean War
she volunteer to go
and even when de British said no
she still brave the Russian snow
a healing star
among the wounded
a yellow sunrise
to the dying

Dem tell me
Dem tell me wha dem want to tell me
But now I checking out me own history
I carving out me identity

Toussaint L'Ouverture Acknowledges Wordsworth's Sonnet 'To Toussaint L'Overture'

I have never walked on Westminster Bridge

or had a close-up view of daffodils.

My childhood's roots are the Haitian hills

where runaway slaves made a freedom pledge

and scarlet poincianas flaunt their scent.

I have never walked on Westminster Bridge

or speak, like you, with Cumbrian accent.

My tongue bridges Europe to Dahomey.

Yet how sweet is the smell of liberty

when human beings share a common garment.

So thanks, brother, for your sonnet's tribute.

May it resound when the Thames' text stays mute.

And what better ground than a city's bridge

for my unchained ghost to trumpet love's decree.

Windrush Child

Behind you
Windrush child
palm trees wave goodbye

above you
Windrush child
seabirds asking why

around you
Windrush child
blue water rolling by

beside you
Windrush child
your Windrush mum and dad

think of storytime yard
and mango mornings

and new beginnings
doors closing and opening

will things turn out right?
At least the ship will arrive
in midsummer light

and you Windrush child
think of grandmother
telling you don't forget to write

and with one last hug
walk good walk good
and the sea's wheel carries on spinning

and from that place England
you tell her in a letter
of your Windrush adventure

stepping in a big ship
not knowing how long the journey
or that you're stepping into history

bringing your Caribbean eye
to another horizon
grandmother's words your shining beacon

learning how to fly
the kite of your dreams
in an English sky

Windrush child
walking good walking good
in a mind-opening
meeting of snow and sun

Crybaby Prime Minister

I'd love to be led
by a crybaby prime minister
who'd burst into tears
whenever people bled

I'd love to be led
by a crybaby prime minister
who'd sob and sob
for everyone without a job

I'd love to be led
by a crybaby prime minister
who'd lose all control
when told of old folks in the cold

I'd love to be led
by a crybaby prime minister
who'd whimper for a while
at the mention of nuclear missile

I'd love to be led
by a crybaby prime minister
who'd suddenly weep
for children with nowhere to sleep

I'd love to be led
by a crybaby prime minister
whose eyes would go red
when trees of the forest are felled

Yes, there's something to be said
for a nation being led
by a crybaby prime minister
who'd reach for a hanky
with a lump in the throat

Such a prime minister
might be worth a vote.

Skin

Is it a window of flesh
to let in the sunlight
and look out at the world?

Is it a wall we wear
to keep others at a distance
and protect our private space?

Is it a frail curtain
for outsiders to puzzle at,
not knowing what's behind?

Is it a birthright billboard
to advertise our race
and declare our allegiance?

Is it mere clingfilm
to wrap blood and bones
beyond our sell-by date?

Is it a bookcover
to contain the heart's
epic loves and hates?

What is this thing, skin?
This dividing screen
that unites the grin

of every skeleton.

A Social Skeleton

I am a skeleton,
my bones are brittle white.
I like to make an entrance
in the dead of night.
See me rattle, see me prance,
see me roll my eyes like dice.
By eyes I mean eye-sockets,
which are all the same to me.

When I enter a room
I bring an unearthly perfume
that always gets me noticed.
Some people stare with looks of ice,
some do their best to be polite.
But being a social skeleton,
I pat the living on the back,
making sure I make eye-contact.

Of course, we skeletons
are not much good at small talk.
When asked about my profession,
I say with charismatic grin:
An expert in putrefaction.
A graduate from the unknown.

Some try to guess my origin,
some marvel at my fleshless bone.

A skeleton, you'll agree,
is the life and soul of a party.
My rib-cage is a sure winner,
my skull a conversation piece.
My ever-grinning demeanour
puts me perfectly at ease
with human flesh of every creed.
Skeletons still feel for those who bleed.

The Giant With A Taste For Mongrel Blood

Fee fi fo fum
I smell the mongrel blood
of the Brit nation.

Be they gentle or be they brute
Be they Pict or be they Jute
Be they Angle or be they Saxon
Be they Roman or be they Dane
Be they fair by trace of Teuton
Be they dark by Moorish strain
Be they Norman with their mouton
Be they West Indian in the vein
Be they of Asian mother tongue
Be they grounded in Celtic Grail
Be they Irish Welsh or Scot
Be they Jew or Huguenot
or the new kid on the block
I'll have the bleeding lot
in my melting pot.
Their mongrel blood will make rich stock.

Behind The Menu

Sweet and Sour
moved in next door
to Fish and Chips.

And farther down the street,
Naan Bread and Curry
were neighbours to Rice and Peas.

But with time, these families
got into a hullabaloo –
or should that be a vindaloo –

when the only boy
of Naan Bread and Curry chose
the Fish and Chips girl to marry.

And the Sweet and Sour youngest
ran off one summer
with the Rice and Peas eldest.

Is there a happy
ending to this story?
That would be telling.

Let's just say they got together
to sort out their grumbles
over apple crumble

and to discuss the loud couple
just moved in to number three –
Bolognese and Spaghetti.

Salt

Once used as Roman currency,
now a common guest at your table.
Sprinkle me over your food and your soul.
I'm known to preserve as well as corrode.
A pinch of me tests the grain of truth.
So spill me if you dare to tempt fate.
In the hands of a Sumo wrestler,
I'm a shower of invocation.
No need to rub me into your wounds.
I'm at home in your sweat and your tears.
Fine or coarse, I can teach you to melt
into the miracle of yourself.

Coal

My body heaved to the hacking of picks.
Fuelled your industry and politics.
I warmed your houses, I stoked your hearth.
Fed you my black carbonaceous heart.
My forsaken pits still send a bitter chill.
Or have you forgotten names like Scargill?
My slumbering slagheaps stalk your history
like the death-song of a canary.
I am the smouldering lump that speaks volumes,
the dark ember glowing in a white room,
a nugget of lost solidarity.

Marriage Of Opposites

I Copper,
child of Fire,
married Zinc,
child of Water,
and gave birth
to a daughter
called Brass.

I Copper,
child of the Sun,
married Tin,
child of the Moon,
and gave birth
to a son
called Bronze.

I Copper,
proud parent
of peaceful bell
and flaming sword,
have many
a story
to tell.

Notes

P.37 Ogun – the Yoruba god of iron, who also figures in Caribbean folk religion.

Nansi (Anansi) – the shape-shifter, creator, trickster-spider of West African and Caribbean lore.

P.56 From a Sebastiáo Salgado photograph, taken in central Bosnia. Part of the Brazilian photographer's epic exhibition, 'Migrations; humanity in transition', held at the Barbican gallery.

P.57 Written to accompany film footage of 'Médicin Sans Frontiéres'.

P.60 Toussaint L'Ouverture – a revolutionary slave leader who opened the way for Haiti to become the first black republic in 1804.

Nanny – a Jamaican national heroine who led runaway slaves to establish a free colony in the hills.

Caribs – the Amerindian tribe from whom the Caribbean got its name.

Mary Seacole – a Jamaican nurse who did not receive the acclaim that Florence Nightingale did, but who put her skills to pioneering use in the Crimean War (1853-6).

P.63 Best known for his daffodils poem, Wordsworth, in the aftermath of the French Revolution, wrote a sonnet about Toussaint L'Ouverture, who was imprisoned in France and died there.

P.64 Empire Windrush; the arrival of this ship in 1948 is a significant landmark in post-war Caribbean migration. A number of the passengers had served in Britain during the war.

'Windrush Child' was inspired by Vince Reid, the youngest Windrush passenger, aged 13 at the time.